A Cat Lover's Guide to Increase Your Credit Score in 90 Days or Less- Guaranteed!

By: HeavenSalter

I0440623

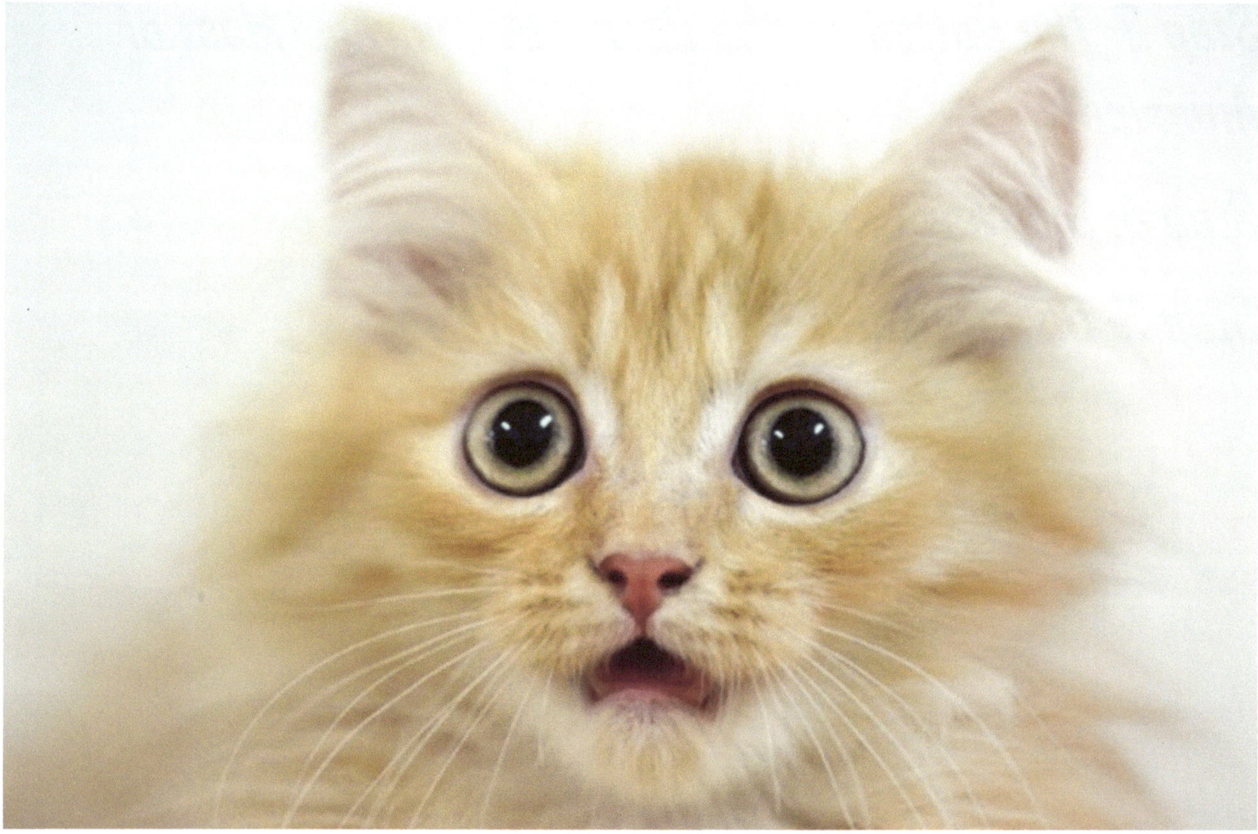

Table of Contents:

Introduction:

Don't you think it would have been relevant to have been taught about your credit score and best practices back in high school? The real "report card" in life that matters, is your credit score. I believe this is a critical life skill we all need to learn at an early age. If we are not taught how to manage money or how to spend responsibly then we are placed in a financial trap. I know we all have done it. It is sort of a rite of passage that we all just have to get into debt at a young age, just to try and get out of it in our later years. You can't live with the "would of", "could of" and "should of's" of life. What we can do is get educated and start fresh and this book is all about helping you start over, no matter what credit situation you are in right now.

As soon as most of us turn 18 we run to our favorite store and get a department store card. It is so exciting to have that first credit card and what do we do-start shopping right away! The sales people do a mighty fine job at making you feel that you can't live without that purchase. They say,"Hey you deserve it!". We don't deserve financial ruin though! We get so excited that our first adult thing we can do besides getting a job, is getting a credit card. We are not warned that if we don't know how to effectively spend, it will hurt us later in life. That is why you are here, right now. You are in a place in your life where you almost want to give up on your credit situation and you have no choice but to accept your current circumstances.

Right now, what you want to learn about it is how to improve your existing credit score and or get a higher credit score. You are going to be surprised just how easy it really is. This quick short guide will tell you exactly what you need to do in order to fix your existing credit score, get new credit and raise your credit score so that you can get a loan or buy a house or just have a great "report card". Before we go into how it is done let's talk a little about credit and what it is and how it works. You can't move towards the future until you have accepted your past and learn from it. So, let's begin shall we.

<u>Step 1-Understanding your Credit Score</u>

A credit score is a numeric system used in order to evaluate your credit worthiness to lenders aka banks and employers. Yes, even employers check your credit score nowadays. They want to make sure you won't steal from them. Believe it or not a bad credit score indicates to your employer that you may have a hardship and you are a security risk! Most importantly your credit score pretty much rates how responsible you will be with other people's money and if you take your finances seriously. On paper anyways. These are the components and percentages that calculate your credit score:

1.Payment History-Are you paying your bills on time? (35%)

2.Amount Owed-The amount of debt or credit used.(30%)

3.Length of Credit History- The length of time you have established credit (15%)

4.New Credit-Will anyone lend you new credit?(10%)

5.Types of Credit used-What are you buying credit for? Vehicle? Clothing etc.(10%)

These are the categories they rate you in and there is a secret formula inside this concept that will help you build credit correctly or fix troubled credit.

Now for your actual credit score. These are the numbers assigned to credit worthiness. Just like you would get an A in school for excellent work you will be assigned a numeric number that tells the world how good of a "student" you are financially in life. Here are the ranges:

Excellent: 750+   You Graduated with Honors with this score!

Good:700-749   Not Bad a B+ is Second Place!

Fair:650-699   Hmmm You May need a Tutor. C's may get degrees but they are a warning sign to most creditors!

Poor:550-649   Wow, Are you Dropping out of school? D

Bad:550-Below   Well I'm sorry to say, Better luck next year!

You Failed!

Your credit score gets monitored regularly by potential lenders or when you apply for new credit. There are three major credit reporting agencies. They each report monthly and they report different things on your credit report. That is why, most creditors will check all three or 1 in specific. You will notice all credit bureaus do not have direct contact phone numbers. You call and it is usually a recording telling you to go to their website. They are no dummies. They want to make things difficult for you. They do everything the long way. The only good thing is. Now, thanks to modern times and technology; you can submit forms online. Credit bureaus now charge you for monthly access to your accounts. You can however get a free credit report once a year by going here: https://www.annualcreditreport.com. There is also myfreecreditreport.com.

Experian

P.O. Box 4500

Allen, TX 75013

Equifax Information Services, LLC

P.O. Box 740256

Atlanta, GA 30348

TransUnion, LLC

Consumer Dispute Center

P.O. Box 2000

Chester, PA 19016

Experian

(888) 397-3742

Equifax

(866) 349-5191

TransUnion, LLC

(800) 916-8800

Now I know I am making light of the situation but in reality guys it is just a number. It should not define you and it isn't too late to turn things around. That's why you are here, right?

To sum it up, your shopping and pay back patterns, indicate to your lenders how well you can pay them back and if you are responsible and if you deserve a reward or if they should kick you out of their "privilege" to lend to club!

Step 2- What matters the Most?

Ok, so now you know how you are being "judged". Like they say it's not Personal-It's Business! That's really what it is all about. How to play the game and win. Let's talk about how to maintain a good score- if you haven't fallen off the bandwagon yet.

Let's say you are in the A-B range or Good to Excellent you probably don't need me to give you any advice. However, wouldn't increasing that score be fun?? I mean has anyone reached 850?? Is there a secret penthouse number of 950 we don't know about? In order to increase your score to its highest rating, you need to pay your bills ahead of time, keep a low balance-Not Zero. Creditors want to make money off you so give them their interest charges but be smart about it. You already know debt to income ratio is the most important thing here so let us move on to what matters most for those of us Not in this category.

Second place is the First to lose!

But aren't we all winners? So, you are part of the C-D category and you are going down the slippery slope of being considered bad credit. Remember you are not a bad person-you just need a personal assistant to keep you on track. If you are in the C category 650-699 you are still ok. You may not have the best interest rates or best special offers but you are doing pretty good. You might have a high debt to income ratio and you may have made a few late payments but you are still way above water. It only takes a 620 credit score in order to be approved for a mortgage and in some cases and some states 590!!! So if you are in this category you just really want to increase your score enough to get better deals and interest rates.

The way to do this- <u>First call your creditors.</u>

Explain to them you have been a good customer and that you want to be reevaluated for an increase in credit or a lower rate. You will be surprised how easy this is and how willing they are to do so.

When you spend more they make more. It is a Win-Win in their eyes.

<u>Next get New credit.</u> This will increase your worth to them. Ultimately the idea is to have the least amount of credit cards with the

highest amount of credit loaned but that's the secret that the A-B excellent credit category has achieved and knows about. So if you're in the C-D category you probably have a lot of credit cards and high balances but you can manage this and you can increase your score by doing these simple things:

1. *Lower your interest rate or Get higher credit amount.* Call the Creditors individually for each type of credit in order to do this.

2. *Get More credit but keep next to nothing balance on this new credit.* Use the Shopping trick method for new credit and only charge what you can afford to pay back according to your set budget.

3. *Monitor your credit so that you can wipe off old debt or incorrect information.* This alone can increase your credit score from 5-10 points if done properly.

4. *Never close out good accounts*!! You need the credit history to work for you!!

5. *Always pay on time and keep your balances low or pay off your bill entirely in 30 days.*

6. *Don't get too much credit and or inquiries on your credit.* This is important because it is easy to get caught up in the fun and excitement of getting approved for so much credit. You want to set a monthly budget of what you can afford to pay back. If your credit card monthly payments combined exceed this, then you have too many! Get it in control so you don't fall back into the mess that pushed you to seek help in the first place. Also, inquiries against your credit occur anytime you apply for new credit. Only apply for the credit you need once you have started all over.

7. *Check your credit score every month from all 3 bureaus.* CreditKarma is a great website I use to monitor my credit and it's

FREE!

https://www.creditkarma.com

Other Resources;

1. www.freecreditreport.com
2. https://www.annualcreditreport.com
3. www.freescoreonline.com

You can always go directly to each creditor to get a free credit report.

1. www.experian.com/consumer-products/free-credit-report.html
2. https://www.transunion.com/annual-credit-report
3. https://www.equifax.com/personal

Step 3-The Bottom of the Barrel Borrowers-Most of America!

You made it! Welcome most of America! The economy has really done a number on jobs and wages and that's why when It comes to putting things into perspective and priority paying credit card bills is the least of our worries when we are trying to survive. I hear you. I've been there myself and I have gotten out of it and that's why I wrote this book.

Ok so, if you are in this category of Bad Credit then you know you have been struggling for a while. There is no need to deny it and you shouldn't feel bad about it because you are not alone in this. Check the statistics you will see that this is almost the norm in most states. States have had to adapt to us now, and that's why they have lowered credit score approvals. Otherwise they wouldn't get any new business!

So how do you get out of this rut? Well for this one I spent a lot of time researching and trial and error myself until I discovered the secret sneaky method I am going to reveal to you right now.

We all know by now that the key to a great credit score is to pay your bills on time, keep your balances low and get new credit plus monitor your credit so you can fix errors that arise. So what do we do when all is almost lost?

You have to fight back and start over pretty much in a creative way.

This is what you must do and I guarantee If you follow these steps you will raise out of that gutter and start to feel hope again. Now I am not saying this is easy or fast but if you are diligent and consistent and follow these steps-you will see results.

First Step: Work on eliminating old debt and incorrect information.

You must call the credit report agencies in order to fix wrong information like your address, past employment etc. To eliminate old debt you can do this right online through each creditor. Go to each one: Equifax, Trans Union and Experian. Pay if you have to. The most they charge is $29-$39 a month for monitoring but this way they will respond quicker because you are a member and you can keep track better as well.

After 7 years most old debt will "fall off". These are the ones I want you to attack. Anything 7 years or older still reporting on your credit file that is bad debt-Start the process of investigation and get it taken off! They must respond within 30 days. Do this first!!! Get going right now and don't keep reading until you have finished this task!

The process is simple. You would login to each creditor and view your credit report. Go to your accounts section and click on the credit information you want to dispute. You will then be redirected to a form that asks you the reason for the dispute. You click on the reason or write a statement and then click dispute. They will send that over to the reporting agency to begin the claim/dispute process.

Example:

See an error?

DIRECT DISPUTE™

If there's an error on your report, you can submit a dispute without leaving Credit Karma.

DISPUTE AN ERROR

Second Step: Start Paying your Active credit on time.

From this day forth DO NOT pay late. Most creditors give you a grace period of 5 days before they assess a late fee and most won't report you as being late unless it has been 31 days. You can even set up payment arrangements where they will post date a payment so you don't incur late fees. However, don't push it. Pay early or at least on the due date. You may ask why I didn't put this as the first step. It's because you want to start the clock on step 1 because, there is waiting period involved and It is a critical step. So, don't procrastinate! When you pay on time on your current credit this will show your creditors that you are taking your credit seriously and are respecting it. This also will get you perks in the future. Things such as higher credit limits and lower interest rates. It will feel a heck of a lot better when You are in control-not your creditors!

Third Step: Get New Credit.

You may be saying to yourself but who is going to give me credit and why should I get more in debt. The answer is simple. New credit washes out old bad credit in a way and will increase your credit score.

There are two ways of getting new credit. One way is to get a Secured card. You can do this with your bank. It is pretty much credit that is guaranteed by your money. Any amount you put in is the amount that your credit amount will be.

I suggest no less than $200 but more realistically make it $500. Remember this is already your money you are using as collateral but it will be reported as new credit and will help improve your credit score. Also, approval is guaranteed.

The next way to get new credit is to do the "shopping trick" technique.

There are several banks and creditors that do pre-approval offers to get new customers. The way this works is, you go to a website and when the pop up appears to register your email-you do, and you register an account. Now you must put something in your cart and then hit checkout. At this moment, if the creditor participates in this pre-approval method you will see a pop up window while you are in the process of checking out that says you are pre-approved for a credit card and apply.

How did they do this? When you first registered, they did a "soft pull" on your credit and decided if you would qualify. A soft pull Is when they run your credit without it counting against your credit score. Keep in mind that it will show up as an inquiry on your report and this does impact your score, but very little.

Here are some creditors that I have had success with doing this method for new credit: Most of them are from Commenity Bank and Synchrony Bank

1. <u>Bontons</u>-Department Store(580)
2. <u>The Limited</u>-Clothing Store(565)
3. <u>Victorias Secret</u>-Although they have raised their approval score to (600)
4. <u>Express</u>-Department Store-(580)
5. <u>Abercrombie & Fitch</u>
6. <u>Ann Taylor</u>
7. <u>Bath & Body Works</u>
8. <u>Brylane Home</u>
9. <u>Buckle</u>
10. <u>Coldwater Creek</u>
11. <u>Express</u>
12. <u>Gamestop</u>
13. <u>HSN</u> (you need to go to the end of the checkout process before it'll appear)
14. <u>J.Crew</u>

15. <u>Jessica London</u>
16. <u>JJill</u>
17. <u>King Size Direct</u>
18. <u>Loft</u>
19. <u>Motorola</u>
20. <u>MyPoints</u>
21. <u>New York & Company</u>
22. <u>One Stop Plus</u>
23. <u>Overstock</u>

And more…just look for credit and department cards issued from those two banks to get the most success. Also, you won't get a lot of credit mostly $250-$500 but it's all you need to have new credit and improve your score.

Another way to get credit is from mail order catalogs.

Some of them are:

1.<u>Ginnys</u>- Online merchandise catalog

2.<u>Midnight Velvet</u>- Women's clothing and home decor

3.<u>Fingerhut</u>- General merchandise and electronics

4.<u>Country Door</u>

5.<u>Stoneberry</u>

6.<u>Seventh Avenue</u>

7.<u> Overstock</u>

8.<u>Monroe and Main</u>

9.<u>KJordan</u>

10.<u>Venus</u>

Fourth Step-Take it upon yourself to report good credit!

You can now report your rent as credit. This is a new thing but if you pay your rent on time this can help you build credit as well. Also remember that each creditor reports different things and they each score you differently. So, if you notice you have a high score in one of them and they are missing some of your creditors then call and report it. You reporting it and adding it to your file, will show up again as new credit or established credit with them. This will increase your score.

Here are two companies that help with reporting your rent to the credit bureaus. The only way to do this is through these companies or through your rental community if they offer the service.

RentTrack.com　　　　　**and**　　　　　**RentReporter.com**

Dispute Letter Sample and Templates!

<mark>Credit Dispute Sample Letter</mark>:

Date
Your Name
Your Address
Your City, State, Zip Code

Complaint Department
Name of Credit Bureau
Address
City, State, Zip Code

To Whom it may concern:

I am writing to dispute the following information in my file. The items I dispute also are encircled on the attached copy of the report I received.

This item (identify item(s) disputed by name of source, such as creditors or tax court, and identify type of item, such as credit account, judgment, etc.) is (inaccurate or incomplete) because (describe what is inaccurate or incomplete and why). I am requesting that the item be deleted (or request another specific change) to correct the information.

Enclosed are copies of (use this sentence if applicable and describe any enclosed documentation, such as payment records, court documents) supporting my position. Please reinvestigate this (these) matter(s) and (delete or correct) the disputed item(s) as soon as possible.

Sincerely,

Your name

Letter to Settle Your Debt and Remove from Credit Report

Name of Creditor
Address
City, St. zip

Re: Collection Account for Original Creditor Account XXXXXXXXX
Amount: $XXX.XX

To Whom it may concern,
I am disputing the validity of the debt referred to above. I am not aware of the account number and you have not informed me of the existence of this account.
I am willing to pay this account IN FULL (or a settlement percentage, whichever is feasible) if you agree to immediately delete the account from the credit reporting agencies (namely Equifax, TransUnion and Experian) that you have reported to, and validated this account. My sole purpose is to get this item removed from my file. This letter should not be interpreted as recognition of the debt or acknowledgment of liability for the debt.
If you accept the terms of this agreement, the certified amount of $XXX will be sent to your collection agency provided there is complete deletion of any reference to the debt from my file on all the credit bureaus that you have reported to, and the debt is validated. As the full amount demanded will be paid back, there should not be any waiting period to delete this item from the reporting bureaus.
Your agency should delete all information regarding the account from my credit files within 10 business days from the receipt of the payment, as mentioned in this agreement. The terms of this agreement will not be discussed with anyone but the original creditor. No third party will be informed if contacted and no acknowledgment of the debt, any kind of payment, or settlement will be discussed if I am contacted by the Reporting Agencies.
Following the acceptance of the agreement, please prepare a letter on your company letter head unambiguously agreeing to the aforementioned terms and conditions and have it signed by your agency's authorized signatory. This letter will imply a legal contract, enforceable under my state law.
If I do not receive an approval letter within 15 days of your receipt of this letter, I will withdraw this offer.
Please communicate regarding this account to the address mentioned below
Your Name
Address
City, St. Zip

Ok so that's it!! I recommend that you focus on one step at a time. Don't rush this process. Miracles don't happen overnight. I also Guarantee that if you did ALL of these things and your score didn't increase by at least 10 points-then you did something wrong or you missed a step.

Trust me. I was my own guinea pig and I was my own student. By following these 4 steps when I had a low 435 credit score in 4 months I was able to raise it 605 and that was a year ago. My credit score now is in the mid 700's and I own two businesses and constantly get new credit offers and loan offers because of this!

You can do this. What helped me the most was getting rid of old credit and getting new credit through the shopping trick method. Those two things alone, increased my score by 75 points!!!!! I once saw my credit score increase by 5 points in 1 week! It all depends on how fast your creditors report things. That brings me to one final point and strategy. Call those creditors and demand they report your good credit ASAP not every couple of months! Stay on top of them just like they stay on top of you when you pay late!

There you have it folks, the sneaky easy method to improving your credit score and rebuilding your financial situation. You are capable of this and these methods work. Of course, everyone will have different results and just because I had great success doesn't mean you will increase your score by 75 points or more right away.

However, it does mean that you **WILL** increase your score and you can increase it enough to buy a house or just be at peace with your finances. Please share your success with me. I look forward to hearing about your secret tricks and of your progress and achievements using this method.

Wishing you all the Best!

Heaven Salter

Email: heavensalter@gmail.com with results and receive a Free Financial Planner.